Hello.

# the BIG ME Little You book

## a journal for kids big and small

Rachel Kempster

Meg Leder

sourcebooks

Art on page vii, 167, courtesy of Clara Leder
Art on page 15, courtesy of Matthew Barry
Art on page 28, 29, 33, 53, 73, 113, courtesy of Teddy Eck
Art on page 96, courtesy of Julia Young
Art on page 115, courtesy of Ella Tuite
Art on page 159, courtesy of Delaney Kempster
Art on page 178, courtesy of Lorelei Eck

This publication is designed to provide accurate and authoritative information in regard to the subject matter covered. It is sold with the understanding that the publisher is not engaged in rendering legal, accounting, or other professional service. If legal advice or other expert assistance is required, the services of a competent professional person should be sought. —*From a Declaration of Principles Jointly Adopted by a Committee of the American Bar Association and a Committee of Publishers and Associations*

Published by Sourcebooks, Inc.
P.O. Box 4410, Naperville, Illinois 60567-4410
(630) 961-3900
Fax: (630) 961-2168
www.sourcebooks.com

Library of Congress Cataloging-in-Publication data is on file with the publisher.

Printed and bound in the United States of America.
VP 10 9 8 7 6 5 4 3 2 1

To Donovan, Clara, Delaney, and
Jack, the best Little Yous we know.

When my niece Clara was born, I happy cried for about three hours straight. I couldn't believe my little brother had a beautiful daughter, that he and my sister-in-law named her after our grandmother, that there was a new tiny person in the world related to me.

And then, a little less than three years later, I was lucky enough to get a nephew too: Jack—a round-faced, smiley little boy who sent me into fits of happy crying yet again.

Now nine and six, Clara and Jack are, hands-down, my favorite people in the world. They are sweet and hilarious and weird and great, and each time I see them, I love them more. Even though I miss them being sweet little toddlers who'd eagerly hop on my lap to share a book, I've also loved watching them grow into the fully realized people they're becoming.

But here's the thing: I don't get to see them much. I live in Brooklyn, New York; they live in Cincinnati, Ohio. It's a little too far to drive in a weekend, and so I have to be content with phone calls and occasional visits. But sometimes, that isn't enough.

And so, for Clara's seventh birthday, I bought her a big blank book that we could share. I filled the first fifteen or so pages with our favorite pictures, a birthday greeting, and questions for her. A few months later, I got it back in the mail, with new pictures, a great page of stickers, and a letter from Clara inside.

We've been mailing the book back and forth for the past two years. (And when Jack turns seven, he'll get one too.) It has become a shared volume of love, a way to stay connected and to know each other better, no matter the distance.

*The Big Me, Little You Book* is meant to be the same thing for you. Whatever your role—grandparent, aunt, uncle, mom, dad, babysitter, nanny, cousin, big sibling—you can use it with the little one in your life. Fill it out in one big rush, or come to it over time. If you don't live close to each other, that's okay—fill out bits at a time and send it to each other in the mail (getting a package is fun!). Then, when you do get to see each other, fill out some of the pages together! And feel free to make the book work for you—skip around, rewrite the prompts, color instead of write, add your own ideas. What's important is that you do it together…whether it be in person or long distance, like Clara and me.

Happy reading, writing, coloring, pasting, talking, laughing, and more…

XO,

Meg

FILL IN YOUR NAMES HERE:

This is the date we started
*The Big Me, Little You Book*:

This is the date we finished
*The Big Me, Little You Book*:

List all the ways you're alike.

List all the ways you're different.

Everyone needs a pick-me-up now and then.

Fill these pages with compliments for each other.

"I wish I could switch places with her for just one day."

*—Freaky Friday*

In the movie *Freaky Friday*, a mother and daughter switch places, becoming the other person for the day. What would your day be like if you both switched places? What would you want to do and see the most? What would you miss about being you?

You show up. —Michelle H.

I love big kids. I share with them. —James, 3

Bake and cook for them to get into their belly! —Melanie H.

Do unexpected thoughtful things for them. My grandma showed us love by cooking and baking special things for us. I still remember the individual apple pies she made for me and my cousin. —Karen K.

Give them roses. —Thomas, 10

Postcards, hand holding, crying, and laughing with them. Really, though, I can never find enough good ways to show people I love them. —Candace M.

I hug them. —Delaney, 8

By showing up every day, and trying to do my best for them. I live for myself, of course, but a true love is someone who expands your definition of the self. My wife and both of my kids are just as important as I am, because from where I sit they are part of me. —Aron G.

You get them flowers, you do nice things, and you hang out with each other. —Clara, 9

You give them hugs and kisses and tickle their belly. —Teagan, 3

I like to do little things to make them happy, sending random notes or letters, sending flowers, buying them a cup of coffee, just something that lets them know I am thinking of them. —Becky F.

# LIST ALL THE WAYS YOU CAN SHOW SOMEONE THAT YOU LOVE THEM.

What does my name mean?

What does your name mean?

What is the history behind our names?

If you could change your first name, would you? What would you change it to? If not, why not? Why do you think your name perfectly suits you?

**ME:**

**YOU:**

Constellations are patterns of stars that tell stories in the sky.
Create your own constellations—patterns that symbolize things
you both love. Make your shared night sky here.

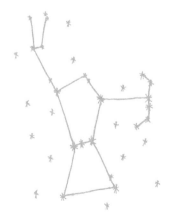

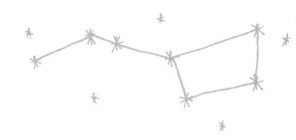

Volunteering can be so much fun. You can meet nice people and do something to help your community. If you love animals, see if the local animal shelter needs help walking dogs. Or maybe you'd like to try making a lemonade stand and donating the money you raise to your school library.

Log your volunteer experiences here. Rate them from 1 to 5, and when you find the one you love the most, keep doing it together.

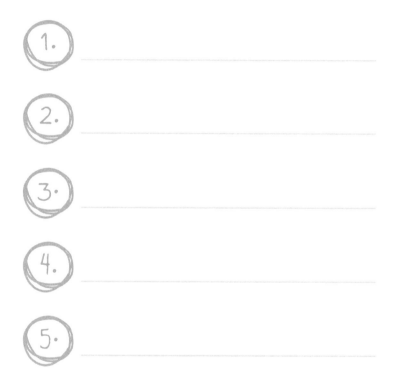

1.

2.

3.

4.

5.

"So please, oh PLEASE, we beg, we pray, Go throw your TV set away, And in its place you can install, A lovely bookshelf on the wall."

**—Roald Dahl, *Charlie and the Chocolate Factory***

Together, make it through a whole day without turning on the TV. Here are some fun things you can do instead:

* Find a duck pond and feed some ducks.

* Make something delicious for lunch together. Fancy grilled cheese or make-your-own pizzas!

* Listen to music together. Take turns sharing your favorite songs.

* Get a big box of crayons and draw. Try to use every color.

* Write a comic book together.

* Go outside and look for cool rocks or sticks or leaves.

* Take a long walk around your neighborhood.

* Go on a bike ride.

* Play catch or fly a kite or challenge each other to a game of Frisbee.

⭐ 15 ⭐

Who are the friends you've heard each other talking about? Fill in the following, then plan a time to meet each other's favorite people. Get to know the people your loved one loves.

|  | YOU | ME |
|---|---|---|
| BEST FRIEND | | |
| OLDEST FRIEND | | |
| FUNNIEST FRIEND | | |
| YOUR FAVORITE THING TO DO WITH FRIENDS | | |
| YOUR FAVORITE QUALITY IN A FRIEND | | |
| MY FRIENDS WOULD DESCRIBE ME AS | | |

A picture of me meeting your friends:

A picture of you meeting my friends:

When I look at you, I think you take after…

Now, it's your turn. Who do I take after?

"Great heroes need great sorrows and burdens, or half their greatness goes unnoticed. It is all part of the fairy tale."

—*The Last Unicorn*

# WHO IS YOUR HERO?

**Who was your hero when you were growing up? Tell me about him/her.**

"A garden is a grand teacher. It teaches patience and careful watchfulness; it teaches industry and thrift; above all it teaches entire trust."

**—Gertrude Jekyll**

Plant something together. Start with seeds, and watch your project grow. Track its progress here.

If you won a million dollars and had to use it to help others,
what would you do?

**You:**

**Me:**

A B C D E F G H I J K L M N O P Q R S T U V W X Y Z

Magnificent, glittery, wow—what are your favorite words? Spend time going through magazines and newspapers cutting out your favorite words. They can look cool, sound cool, have cool definitions—your choice! Paste them here. Fill the pages in one sitting, or add to them as time goes by!

A B C D E F G H I J K L M N O P Q R S T U V W X Y Z

ABCDEFGHIJKLMNOPQRSTUVWXYZ

ABCDEFGHIJKLMNOPQRSTUVWXYZ

# MAKE BUBBLES TOGETHER!

What you'll need:

**1 cup water**
**½ cup liquid dish soap**
**2 teaspoons white sugar**

(If you want more bubbles, double or triple the recipe as needed.)
Mix everything together and then experiment with different objects
to see what makes the best bubble wand. Try cookie cutters, a fly
swatter, a wire wisk, and even a straw (make sure you blow out,
not in).

"If you could only sense how important you are to the lives of those you meet; how important you can be to the people you may never even dream of. There is something of yourself that you leave at every meeting with another person."

—**Fred Rogers**

What parts of yourself do you share with others? Your happy smile? Your good jokes? Your kindness? Write a list of the best bits of you that you want to share with all the people you meet.

**ME:**

**YOU:**

Fill in the chart below, and compare your answers. How are you the same? How are you different?

| DATE: | YOU | ME |
|---|---|---|
| FAVORITE TV SHOW | | |
| FAVORITE MOVIE | | |
| FAVORITE ACTOR OR ACTRESS | | |
| FAVORITE SONG | | |
| FAVORITE BAND OR SINGER | | |

Fill this out again, a year from when you first filled it out. How have you changed? What stayed the same?

| DATE: | YOU | ME |
|---|---|---|
| FAVORITE TV SHOW | | |
| FAVORITE MOVIE | | |
| FAVORITE ACTOR OR ACTRESS | | |
| FAVORITE SONG | | |
| FAVORITE BAND OR SINGER | | |

# If you were an animal, what kind of animal would you be? Why?

A Border Collie with my very own farm! It would be great fun to work hard and play hard on a scenic farm. Completely carefree. —Angela G.

I would love to be a dog because dogs are my favorite animal and most all dogs have good lives. —Lorelei, 10

A kitten so I could fall asleep at any moment and not be judged. —Melanie H.

A dragon. They are awesome and can breathe fire. —Madelyn, 11

A bug. Because I wanna go fast. Because I wanna go slow. —James, 3

I would be an owl because the can fly, see in the dark, and are always saying smart things. —Candace M.

Leopard because I like to stay hidden until I have a chance at doing something. —Aiden, 10

A giraffe, because they are really cute, they are vegetarians and I am vegetarian just like one and so, I would really like to be a giraffe. —Vimmy, 7

A leopard, because they're the most graceful of all the big cats, and they have beautiful spots and are really pretty to see at night when they are hunting. —Thomas, 10

A wolf, because they are beautiful, mate for life, and live in family packs. —Monisha P.

A zebra because I like my zebra shirt. —Delia, 6

I would be a tiger because sometimes they have a nice roar. —Collin, 3

# IF YOU COULD BE ANY ANIMAL, WHAT WOULD IT BE?

Try to guess each other's animals! Draw your animals here.

Who's your favorite teacher of all time? It could be your kindergarten teacher or your karate teacher. What did you learn from them? Why do they mean so much to you?

**YOU:**

**ME:**

# FILL IN THE TITLES OF YOUR VERY FAVORITE BOOKS.

YOU:

ME:

* Meg's favorites are *Alexander and the Terrible, Horrible, No Good, Very Bad Day*; *Anne of Green Gables*; and *Harriet the Spy*. Rachel's favorites are: *Where the Sidewalk Ends*; *All of a Kind Family*; and *Anna to the Infinite Power*.

Write a quick letter to the other person, right here, right now.
No need for a special occasion—just say hello.

# DRAW PICTURES OF THE FOOD YOU HATED TO EAT WHEN YOU WERE LITTLE.

YOU:

ME:

Rachel's mom won't eat green food since eating a bad batch of pistachio ice cream as a kid. Meg's friend Megan won't mix fruit with meat. We all have funny rules about food. Share yours with each other and write them out below.

**Name:**

An eagle OR a robin?

Why? *there Brave*

A cat OR a dog?

Why? *there cute*

A mountain OR an ocean?

Why?

The sun OR the moon?

Why?

An actor OR an astronaut?

Why?

A city dweller OR a country resident?

Why?

Name:

## Would you rather be...

An eagle **OR** a robin?

Why?_____

A cat **OR** a dog?

Why?_____

A mountain **OR** an ocean?

Why?_____

The sun **OR** the moon?

Why?_____

An actor **OR** an astronaut?

Why?_____

A city dweller **OR** a country resident?

Why?_____

Visit another country without ever leaving your hometown! What is a country you'd both like to visit? Write it here:

Now, spend time researching the country together. Find out what traditions and holidays the people embrace, and their favorite foods and dress. What are the best places to visit in the country, and what is the weather like?

Try a restaurant that celebrates the country's cuisine, or make a food that's associated with the country.

Once you've finished, record the details here. What did you like best about the country? Would you want to live there? Why or why not?

If I'm feeling blue, I make a hand turkey. I always have a piece of paper and a pen. I'm not very good at drawing in the eyes or the beak, but it never fails to cheer me up!

—Rachel

Make a whole family of hand turkeys using markers and glue and googly eyes and feathers. You can wait until Thanksgiving to do it, but then you're missing out on a lot of fun!

Write the name of your turkey family here:

```
┌─────────────────────────────────────────────┐
│                                               │
│                                               │
│                                               │
│                                               │
│                                               │
└─────────────────────────────────────────────┘
```

*Some good turkey names: Mr. Gobbles, Feather Featherbody, Tom, Bawk Bawk. But I bet you can do even better.

What's the thing that you do best? Tying shoelaces fast, making cheese sandwiches, playing Go Fish? Choose the one thing you do best, and show me how to do it. Write down the hardest part of doing that thing, and the easiest part.

My turn—now I'm going to teach you how to _____.
What's the hardest part? What's the easiest part?

Fill in the chart below, and compare your answers. How are you the same? How are you different?

| DATE: | YOU | ME |
|---|---|---|
| FAVORITE DAY OF THE WEEK | | |
| LEAST FAVORITE DAY OF THE WEEK | | |
| FAVORITE MONTH | | |
| FAVORITE SEASON | | |
| FAVORITE BAND OR SINGER | | |

Fill this out again, a year from when you first filled it out. How have you changed? What stayed the same?

| DATE: | YOU | ME |
|---|---|---|
| FAVORITE DAY OF THE WEEK | | |
| LEAST FAVORITE DAY OF THE WEEK | | |
| FAVORITE MONTH | | |
| FAVORITE SEASON | | |
| FAVORITE BAND OR SINGER | | |

# TAKE TURNS ADDING GRAFFITI TO THIS WALL.

My niece and I invented a board game called "Escape the Pound!" She did all the art and planning, and I helped put together the game board. We turned a rainy day into a fun day by using our imaginations.

—Rachel

It's time to make your own game. Get a big piece of poster board, markers, glue, and construction paper.

 Plan it out:
* ★ What's the game called?
* ★ How many people can play?
* ★ What are the rules?
* ★ How do you win?

 Next, make it:
* ★ Create your game!
* ★ Will there be cards or dice involved?

Draw or tape a picture of it here.

 Ready. Set. PLAY! Play the game you made and see who wins!

Knitting. —Clara, 9

I really wish I had legible handwriting. —Dan K.

Riding a scooter that goes up and down. —Collin, 3

I wish I had the talent of being flexible, I'm one of the least flexible people ever. —Sean C.

Actually, I'm pretty good at everything. —Ella, 9

I wish I could tap dance. —Lori T.

I wish I could be good at math. —Madelyn, 11

Raise one eyebrow like Mr. Spock. —Matthew B.

I wish I was a professional figure skater. —Vimmy, 7

I wish I could kick a football through goalposts 40 and 50 yards away. I'd be able to work for a handful of years and then retire! —Aron G.

To be a good singer. —Delaney, 8

I wish I was the most accurate person in the world for archery. —Thomas, 10

What talents do you each have? Can you make a perfect cup of cocoa? Or draw a horse that actually looks like a horse? List them all, big and small, here.

"We can't take any credit for our talents. It's how we use them that counts."

**—Madeleine L'Engle, *A Wrinkle in Time***

It's hard to remember all the fun things you've done together—so use this page to keep track of it all. Paste in your movie stubs and tickets to plays and admission wristbands to the zoo. Record the date you went and your one favorite memory. ("I liked the movie, but I really liked it when we shared that giant tub of popcorn together!")

Circle the word that describes you best. Pick a different color pen or pencil or crayon for your answers so you can tell them apart. Add up the number of answers you agree on—are you more alike than you are different? Does that surprise you?

Night **OR** Day

Breakfast **OR** Dinner

Pancakes **OR** Waffles

Swimming **OR** Biking

Sunshine **OR** Rain

Strawberry **OR** Banana

Messy **OR** Neat

Chocolate Milk **OR** Plain Milk

Sneakers **OR** Shoes

Loud **OR** Quiet

Reading **OR** Math

Baseball **OR** Football

Robots **OR** Dinosaurs

Peanut Butter **OR** Jelly

Halloween **OR** Thanksgiving

## ME

Night **OR** Day

Breakfast **OR** Dinner

Pancakes **OR** Waffles

Swimming **OR** Biking

Sunshine **OR** Rain

Strawberry **OR** Banana

Messy **OR** Neat

Chocolate Milk **OR** Plain Milk

Sneakers **OR** Shoes

Loud **OR** Quiet

Reading **OR** Math

Baseball **OR** Football

Robots **OR** Dinosaurs

Peanut Butter **OR** Jelly

Halloween **OR** Thanksgiving

FGHIJKLMNOPQRSTUVWXYZ ABCDEFGHIJKLMN

Create a Me and You alphabet of shared memories…record a shared love or event for each letter. Maybe I = IHOP, where you like to go to lunch together, or S = *Star Wars*, a movie you watched together. Write or draw your ideas here.

R S T U V W X Y Z A B C D E F G H I J K L M N O P Q R S T U V W X Y Z

Sure, you can call something blue. But there's also popsicle blue, swimming pool blue, and Cinderella's dress blue. Pick your favorite color, then add every shade of it you can find here...you can use crayons, paint chips, pictures clipped from magazines—whatever represents the color. Now, come up with new names for all the shades you featured.

"Every real story is a never-ending story."

**—Michael Ende, *The NeverEnding Story***

Build a story together. Fill these two blank pages with a story of your creation—it can be funny, scary, happy, or sad. Start with one little sentence, then add another. And another. Keep going until you haven't any more space to write.

## What makes you special?

List five totally unique things about each other.

1.

2.

3.

4.

5.

1. _____

2. _____

3. _____

4. _____

5. _____

Create an elaborate secret handshake only the two of you know. Practice until you know it by heart. Draw the steps here.

These days, we write other people with emails and text messages. But sometimes it's nice to get a hand-written letter in the mail, just for you! Take the time to write each other a message. Mail it, but don't tell the other person when you do—it's more fun to get something if you don't know it's coming!

## If you could have dinner with any famous person (from the past or present), who would it be?

Harriet Tubman. —Angela G.

If I could have dinner with anyone it would be the famous boy band One Direction. —Lorelei, 10

I would have dinner with my mom because she is nice. —Teddy, 7

I would love to have dinner with my grandmother. I have so many questions I never got to ask her. I would love to have just a few minutes to introduce her to my family and ask her the questions I long to have the answers to. —Tracey E.

I would have dinner with Steve Jobs because I've always wondered what went on in his head. —Sean C.

Slash from Guns N' Roses because he has great guitar skills. —Jack, 6

Albus Dumbledore. —Kerry S.

I would pick my grandmother. Even though I spent a ton of quality time with her, there are still a lot of things I would love for her to tell me and teach me. —Lori T.

Elvis. I think there would be some good comfort food and lots of silly jokes. And we probably would watch some television during and/or after dinner. And we probably would wear some comfortable matching track suits. —Jenny C.

Our dog Izzy who died last year. —Elliot, 8

Anne Shirley of Green Gables. We'd drink raspberry cordials and discuss the right shade of red hair for me. —Candace M.

Clara Barton. —Clara, 9

I'd love to have dinner with my grandpa again. I was only 8 when he died, so I'd love to see him again to hear his voice and laughter. As an eight-year-old, I wasn't looking for similarities between us, but now I'd like to know those.
—Rachel O.

Rachel's niece would like to have dinner with Justin Bieber. Meg's niece would rather invite Clara Barton. Tell each other about the famous folks you'd like to have over for spaghetti. They can be someone from the past (George Washington—and fingers crossed he brings a cherry pie!) or present (Big Bird—to see if he's really that tall in person).

What do you want to be when you grow up?

When I was your age, I wanted to be this when I grew up:

☆ 66 ☆

What are you most looking forward to right now? Your birthday? Friday? Christmas? Write it down, along with today's date, and explain your excitement.

**YOU:**

**ME:**

# USE THIS PAGE TO DRAW A PICTURE OF ME. USE AT LEAST FOUR DIFFERENT PENS, MARKERS, CRAYONS, OR PENCILS.

# NOW I'M GOING TO USE THIS PAGE TO DRAW A PICTURE OF YOU USING EVEN MORE COLORS!

When my grandpa (Clara and Jack's great-grandpa!) turned ninety, we had a big family party. Before the surprise party, all of my grandpa's grandkids and great-grandkids made him big birthday signs, wishing him a very happy birthday. They made awesome decorations for an even more awesome party.

— Meg

Spend some time thinking about someone you both love. And then celebrate him or her! Maybe it's a grandparent celebrating a birthday, a sibling who's feeling left out, or a neighbor who's under the weather. Make a cheerful, bright poster for him or her. Take a picture of the happy recipient with their gift and paste it here!

The nicest thing you've ever done for me:

The nicest thing I've ever done for you:

Write a quick letter to the other person, right here, right now.
No need for a special occasion—just say hello.

# GETTING TO KNOW YOU: CHILDHOOD

Fill in your childhood likes below. Were you similar when you were little?

## WHAT I WANTED TO BE

YOU:

ME:

## FAVORITE TOY

YOU:

ME:

## TV SHOW

YOU:

ME:

## HOLIDAY

YOU:

ME:

## SCHOOL SUBJECT

YOU:

ME:

## ACTIVITY

YOU:

ME:

## DINNER

YOU:

ME:

## DESSERT

YOU:

ME:

Fill in the chart below, and compare your answers. How are you the same? How are you different?

| DATE: | YOU | ME |
|---|---|---|
| FAVORITE SPORT TO PLAY | | |
| LEAST FAVORITE SPORT TO PLAY | | |
| FAVORITE ATHLETE | | |
| FAVORITE OLYMPIC SPORT | | |
| ACTIVITY I MOST WANT TO TRY | | |

Fill this out again, a year from when you first filled it out. How have you changed? What stayed the same?

| DATE: | YOU | ME |
|---|---|---|
| FAVORITE SPORT TO PLAY | | |
| LEAST FAVORITE SPORT TO PLAY | | |
| FAVORITE ATHLETE | | |
| FAVORITE OLYMPIC SPORT | | |
| ACTIVITY I MOST WANT TO TRY | | |

Find a place to sit outside together. Get comfortable! Spend the next ten minutes compiling a list of what you each see around you. Don't share lists until the ten minutes are up. Now compare your lists. How many of the same things did you note?

# A happy timeline

Chart the happiest times you've had together here.

Create treasure hunts for each other, hiding clues throughout your homes. What will be at the end? Maybe it's your favorite picture of the both of you, or a card you made just for the other person. Once you're done, glue some of the clues here.

HERE IS A PICTURE OF ME
WHEN I WAS IN FIRST GRADE.

# ADD A PICTURE OF YOU FROM FIRST GRADE.

How do you stop an elephant from charging?
Take away its credit card. —Carol S.

What animal should you never play cards with?
A cheetah. —Neal, 5

Where does a cow go on a date?
To the mooooooovies. —Tracy H.

How can you tell when a train is eating?
You hear it chew, chew, chewing. —Paul, 7

What do monsters eat for dessert?
I scream sandwiches. —Garrett, 4

Why is 6 afraid of 7?
Because 7 ate 9. —Amy C.

Why did dinosaurs die out?
Because their eggs-stink. —Josh, 10

Why do girls wear makeup and perfume?
Because they're ugly and they stink. (It's kind of mean, but it cracks me up!) —Kristen H.

HA! HA! HA!

"Your brain is doing some great work when it's laughing. "

**—Jon Scieszka**

Try to make each other laugh by telling each other your best jokes. Then write down the ones that you made you both laugh the hardest here.

If you could live anywhere in the world (or the universe!), where would it be? What do you think it would be like to live there? What's your favorite thing about the place—the weather, the animals, the people?

# THESE ARE A FEW OF
# OUR FAVORITE THINGS...

It's time to collage! Spend some time looking through magazines, old greeting cards, pictures, and more. Find images you both like and paste them here. Fill the pages up, so there's no blank space left!

Find a local farm or a petting zoo and spend the day
hanging out with the animals. Record the best bits of your day here.

"If you go off into a far, far forest and get very quiet, you'll come to understand that you're connected with everything."

**—Alan Watts**

Shhh. See how long you can be quiet together. Don't read or play or do anything more than sit with your eyes closed. Start with five minutes, ten minutes until you can do it longer. What do you notice when you're not making any noise?

**YOU:**

**ME:**

The things I like best about you are:

What are the things you like best about me?

## If you're having a sad day, what's the one thing guaranteed to cheer you up?

Having my daughter smile at me. —Angela G.

A bedtime story. —Michelle H.

Whenever I'm sad I go for a long bike ride. —Sean C.

If the weatherman and weather agree and we wound up with a week of snow days. —Aiden, 10

Seeing a little dog that thinks it's a big dog. Or seeing a dog that looks a little bit like a pig. —Jenny C.

Pictures of puppies. Or puppies hugging animals that are not other puppies (although that is awesome) like a puppy snuggled up with a piglet or a kitten. —Meredith D.

Um…applesauce. —Zoe, 3

My son's made up jokes. He told us today at dinner: "Why did the chicken cross the road?" I said, "To get to the other side?" He said, "No, to sit on top of a car and lay an egg." —Tina L.

Wandering around the mall. —Alice P.

Monkey, Froggy, and Taggy and when I have a snack. —Collin, 3

*Pride and Prejudice* always, always, always, cheers me up! —Becky F.

Even on your most crabby day, there must be something that cheers you. Petting your dog? Coloring? Fill out this cheer-up prescription so you're prepared to make each other feel better when skies are gray.

# PRESCRIPTION

FOR: _____    FROM: _____

AILMENT: _____    DATE: _____

℞

SPECIAL INSTRUCTIONS

DOSAGE: _____

REFILLS: _____

SIGNATURE

What songs make you smile? Songs that you sing yourself ("You Are My Sunshine")? Or songs that you hear on the radio ("What Makes You Beautiful")? Use this page to list your happy songs.

Not all our memories are warm and fuzzy. On his first visit to
Disney World, my nephew threw up Pringles all over the bed.
It was definitely really gross (really gross!), but it cracks us up
whenever we tell the story!

—Rachel

What are some of your funny gross stories? Did you get sick after riding a
roller coaster? Or fall down in a muddy puddle on a rainy day? Come up with
a list of the silliest, ickiest memories you have.

I love taking silly photos. Ever since my niece and nephew
were born, I've been making them do funny things in front of the
camera. I convinced my nephew to dress up like an elf—more than
once. We've destroyed gingerbread houses on camera, and had
funny-face photo shoots. I love looking through the pictures and
remembering all the silly fun we've had.

—Rachel

Fill these pages with photos from your own silly photo shoots. Here are
some ideas to get you started:

* Get a big piece of butcher paper
  and make a cool backdrop.

* Pretend you're a movie star getting your picture
  taken at your film premiere. Act fancy.

* Take turns acting like your favorite animals.

* Act out all your feelings—sad, happy,
  surprised, mad, hungry, etc.

* Call out different scenarios to each other and snap
  away: You're being chased by a bear! You fell in wet
  cement! You dropped your popsicle!

POST YOUR FAVORITE PICTURES
ON THESE PAGES.

Fill in the chart below, and compare your answers. How are you the same? How are you different?

| DATE: | YOU | ME |
|---|---|---|
| **FAVORITE BOOK** | | |
| **FAVORITE BOOK CHARACTER** | | |
| **THE BOOK CHARACTER WHO IS MOST LIKE ME** | | |
| **THE BOOK I WANT TO READ NEXT** | | |
| **THE BOOK I AM READING NOW** | | |

Fill this out again, a year from when you first filled it out. How have you changed? What stayed the same?

| DATE: | YOU | ME |
|---|---|---|
| **FAVORITE BOOK** | | |
| **FAVORITE BOOK CHARACTER** | | |
| **THE BOOK CHARACTER WHO IS MOST LIKE ME** | | |
| **THE BOOK I WANT TO READ NEXT** | | |
| **THE BOOK I AM READING NOW** | | |

Who are your favorite cartoon characters? Scooby-Doo? Nemo? Lightning McQueen? Take turns drawing your favorites here (and it's OK if they don't look EXACTLY the same!).

1. _____

2. _____

3. _____

4. _____

5. _____

6. _____

7. _____

8. _____

9. _____

10. _____

"The more that you read, the more things you will know. The more you learn, the more places you'll go. "

**—Dr. Seuss**

Start a book club together. Review your bookshelves at home, and write down all the books you'd like to read together (even ones that you read on your own already). Then visit the library or bookstore to add even more books. Now pick your first book and plan a time to talk about it. List the book and date here:

## HERE ARE SOME QUESTIONS YOU CAN ASK EACH OTHER:

- On a scale of 1 to 10, with 10 being the highest, what score would you give this book?
- What did you like about it?
- What didn't you like about it?
- Fill in the following sentence: "If I could be any character from the book, I would be…" Why? How are you like this character and how are you different? Would you do things differently or the same as the character?
- What was your favorite part of the book and why? Read aloud your favorite part.
- Would you tell a friend to read this book? Why or why not?
- How would you re-write the ending of the book—or is it perfect as is?
- If you could ask the author a question, what would it be?
- Do some research together: Is there a sequel to the book? (If there isn't, should there be? What would happen?) Who is the author? Has the author written any other books?

HERE IS A STORY I WROTE ABOUT YOU:

# NOW, YOU WRITE A STORY ABOUT ME:

## IF YOU WERE AN ICE CREAM FLAVOR,

YOU'D BE:

I'D BE:

## IF YOU WERE A SONG,

YOU'D BE:

I'D BE:

## IF YOU WERE A COLOR,

YOU'D BE:

I'D BE:

## IF YOU WERE AN ANIMAL,

YOU'D BE:

I'D BE:

## IF YOU WERE A FOOD,

YOU'D BE:

I'D BE:

## IF YOU WERE A PLACE,

YOU'D BE:

I'D BE:

## IF YOU WERE A PLANT,

YOU'D BE:

I'D BE:

## IF YOU WERE A _____,

YOU'D BE:

I'D BE:

Write a quick letter to the other person, right here, right now.
No need for a special occasion—just say hello.

What's the one thing you can draw the best? Draw it here, and write a little caption under it telling the story of the artist (just like you see at the museum!).

"It's kind of fun to do the impossible. "

**—Walt Disney**

Name one impossible thing that you wish you could do. Flying? Stopping time? Growing ten feet tall every time you eat a cupcake?

**ME:**

**YOU:**

*Point Break*—Keanu is hysterical! —Michelle H.

*Planes, Trains & Automobiles*. I've never seen a movie with so many scenes that make me laugh out loud! —Matthew B.

*Best in Show*: "Walnuts, hickory nuts, pistachios, peanuts…." —Pat L.

*Home Alone*, because the kid is way smarter than his opponents. —Thomas, 10

*Home Alone 2*, because it's just really funny. —Vimmy, 7

*Office Space*. I came of age in Silicon Valley in the 1990s, and I groove on dork humor. —Monisha P.

*Grumpy Old Men*. Because: Walter Matthau. —Alice P.

*Aladdin*. The parrot is loud and silly. —Delia, 6

*Despicable Me*, because when Gru says he has to assemble an army he went and then came back and he hit the minions head with a hammer —Jack, 6

*St. Elmo's Fire* is unintentionally ridiculous. —Ruth E.

*Elf* is one of my all-time favorite funny movies. The scene where Buddy told the department store Santa that he smelled like beef and cheese was the best! —Tina L.

*Con Air* because it's just that bad and Nicolas Cage is in it. —Kerry S.

I LOVE Whoopi Goldberg in *Jumpin' Jack Flash*. If I see it listed—I watch it. —Karen K.

List all the movies that make you laugh here.
Are there any that you disagree on?

In A. S. King's book *Ask the Passengers*, the narrator Astrid spends time sending wishes to people on the airplanes that fly overhead. Carry on her tradition by filling these pages with wishes for other people.

Perhaps you both want to wish that your bus driver gets her favorite cake for her birthday. Or maybe you want to wish that the grocery store clerk hears his favorite song on the radio tonight. Or maybe you see a guy frowning in the street—maybe you want to wish he'll hear a joke that will make him laugh. List your shared wishes here.

One summer, I realized I had never eaten mac and cheese, my
niece Clara's favorite meal. Conversely, Clara had never tried
strawberries, one of my all-time most loved foods. So we decided
to try each other's favorites. Before the big bite, we spent time
telling each other why we liked the food, and then, on the count of
three, we each tried the food in question. And we both agreed that
trying each other's favorite food was a good way to try new things.

— Meg

What are the foods you're each afraid to try? Maybe there's a food neither
of you have tried. List the foods here, and then record your impressions.

**Date:**

**Food:**

**Impression:**

**Verdict:**          Yum          Maybe          No, thanks!

**Date:**

**Food:**

**Impression:**

**Verdict:**          Yum          Maybe          No, thanks!

**Date:**

**Food:**

**Impression:**

**Verdict:**       Yum        Maybe        No, thanks!

**Date:**

**Food:**

**Impression:**

**Verdict:**       Yum        Maybe        No, thanks!

**Date:**

**Food:**

**Impression:**

**Verdict:**       Yum        Maybe        No, thanks!

My niece Clara asked me to take pictures of the buildings I liked
best in NYC. It was a cool request because I had never spent that
much time observing the buildings around me, but once she asked,
I couldn't stop finding things I liked.

— Meg

What buildings do you each like best in the world? Create a city skyline of
your shared favorite buildings. Don't forget to add stars!

Find a good picture of each other's face—a school photo can work well for this. Using a color photo copier, make multiple copies. Cut out the face, but leave the hair out. Now, give each other funky hair styles—use different colors, yarn and glitter, and other supplies. The sky's the limit!

What are your nicknames, favorite inside jokes, and goofy traditions?
List them all here. Add to these pages as you get older.

Make each other a costume using everyday supplies from around the house. Maybe it's a robot outfit made from a box and some aluminum foil. Or it's a gypsy costume created from scarves. The only rule? Whatever the other person makes, you have to wear—no matter how wacky! Add a picture of your costumes here.

Start a shared doodle here. Pass it back and forth. The only rule is you have to start drawing exactly where the other person left off, so that everything is connected in one line. Keep growing your drawing in ways you both might not expect.

My first memory of you was…

What is your first memory of me? Draw or write it here.

Fill in the chart below, and compare your answers. How are you the same? How are you different?

| DATE: | YOU | ME |
|---|---|---|
| **FAVORITE ICE CREAM FLAVOR** | | |
| **FAVORITE PIZZA TOPPINGS** | | |
| **FAVORITE FRUIT** | | |
| **FAVORITE VEGETABLE** | | |
| **FOOD I MOST WANT TO TRY** | | |

Fill this out again, a year from when you first filled it out. How have you changed? What stayed the same?

| DATE: | YOU | ME |
|---|---|---|
| **FAVORITE ICE CREAM FLAVOR** | | |
| **FAVORITE PIZZA TOPPINGS** | | |
| **FAVORITE FRUIT** | | |
| **FAVORITE VEGETABLE** | | |
| **FOOD I MOST WANT TO TRY** | | |

THIS IS MY FAVORITE PICTURE
OF US TOGETHER.

THIS IS YOUR FAVORITE PICTURE
OF US TOGETHER.

Do you ever wonder what it would be like to know each other if you were the same age? Pretend you're the same age and write a letter to each other. If you're eight, pretend the other person is eight. If you're thirty-eight, pretend the other person is thirty-eight. What sorts of things will you talk about? Write your letters here.

Plan a slumber party! Get sleeping bags and extra pillows, eat some fun food, watch a movie, and then turn off the lights and talk too much! Plan your evening here:

What are your favorite songs to sing out loud? Have a sing-along together! Pick some songs that you love and print copies of the lyrics. Now turn on the radio and start singing—the louder the better. List everything you sang here:

What are your biggest strengths? Is it being generous, giving good gifts, or making other people feel included? Write lists of your strengths together—then use them as inspiration to create superhero versions of each other, highlighting those strengths, like Kind-to-Animals Man or Super Always-Helps-Her-Mom Girl!

Design a toy together—draw out your blueprint here. What will it do? What will it be made from? Will it need batteries? What color will it be?

Visit a local natural history museum together! What was the best part? Was anything boring? Did you learn something? Buy a souvenir? Write down all your memories here.

HERE IS A PICTURE OF ME
WHEN I WAS BORN.

ADD A PICTURE OF YOU
WHEN YOU WERE BORN.

Fill in these certificates for each other! For example:

You're a great aunt because you always wish me a happy birthday and you make me feel special.

Best Nana Ever Award: Awarded because you always make the best grilled cheese.

## CERTIFICATE OF MERIT

AWARDED TO:

FOR:

ON THIS DATE:

SIGNED BY:

# ✳✳✳✳

## CERTIFICATE OF MERIT

**Awarded to:**


**For:**



**On this date:**

**Signed by:**

# MAKE A DIORAMA!

You'll need:

* A shoebox
* A wallet-size picture of both of you
* Crayons, markers, assorted art supplies
* Cardboard
* Glue
* Scissors

Decide on a scene you want to create. Maybe you want to replicate the room you're in right now. Or maybe you want to pretend you're both on another planet. Cut out the pictures of your heads, and draw the bodies on cardboard. Glue the head on top.

Now, create your diorama scene. Use your imagination! Cotton balls can be clouds. A tiny jewelry box can be a bed. Spools can make a good kitchen table base. A little felt can represent grass. Have fun!

If you ran a zoo, you'd get to name some of the animals! Rachel would name a hippo her Hungry Hungry Hippo. Meg would name a walrus Bob. Brainstorm names for the animals here:

**Snake:**

**Lion:**

**Owl:**

**Flamingo:**

**Tiger:**

**Penguin:**

**Dolphin:**

**Peacock:**

**Monkey:**

**Hippo:**

**Crocodile:**

**Turtle:**

**Bear:**

**Panda:**

## What would be the most fun vacation you can imagine?

Camping somewhere beautiful and warm! —Melanie H.

Reading by the ocean in Greece. —Ruth E.

A huge house on the beach filled with my favorite people in the world. And a stocked fridge. —Nancy E.

Being in a little, quaint town either in New England or overseas browsing in antique stores, bookstores, and then having a little lunch at a pub. —Pat L.

Going with Grandma and Grandpa. It's in Ohio. We play and sway and we sleep and do everything. —Zoe, 3

Traveling through space and time into the past and seeing every concert I ever wished I saw…like all those Vans Warped tours in the '90s and definitely the Beatles rooftop concert. —Kerry S.

Taking a cruise to Alaska with my family and then driving back home. —Aiden, 10

Traveling with all my nieces and nephews, my brothers and sisters, and my mom to a place we have never been to before. —Becky F.

Hilton Head. —Clara, 9

Another Disney Cruise! —Delaney, 8

DREAM UP THE BEST
VACATION YOU COULD
EVER THINK OF TAKING
TOGETHER, AND PLAN
IT OUT HERE.

My favorite memory of you is:

What is your favorite memory of me?

Create a Me and You flag. Use your favorite colors
and incorporate images that represent the both of you.

Using old magazines and catalogs, build an outfit for the other person. Try to use different pictures: shoes from one page, a sweater from another. The outfit can be cool or wacky, pretty or fun. Paste your ideas here.

## MY OUTFIT FOR YOU:

YOUR OUTFIT FOR ME:

Do you remember the best day you ever had together? What were your favorite things? The place you went, the people you visited, or maybe the food you ate? Imagine you can plan an even BETTER day. A perfect day. Use these pages to plan things from morning to night.

Write a list together of nice things you can do for other people—then go out and do them. We'll get you started:

* Give a flower to your mom.

* Make someone a card.

* Write letters to your friends and mail them out. No emails!

* Help an elderly neighbor.

* Bake some cookies and bring them to your favorite bus driver.

* _____

* _____

* _____

* _____

* _____

* _____

* _____

* _____

Write a quick letter to the other person, right here, right now.
No need for a special occasion—just say hello.

Fill in the following:

When I was your age, my favorite movie was:

Right now, your favorite movie is:

Now, plan a movie night to watch both! Buy your favorite candy or make some popcorn, get comfortable, and enjoy!

My grandpa Mousey was a race car driver, and my grandma and I
would sit in the stands and cheer him on. She'd track the times of
his laps.

—Rachel

Go to a place you love—the bowling alley, the yarn store, the park, etc.
Write about your adventure together here.

Fill in the chart below, and compare your answers. How are you the same?
How are you different?

| DATE: | YOU | ME |
|---|---|---|
| FAVORITE VACATION | | |
| FAVORITE COUNTRY | | |
| FAVORITE PLANET | | |
| FAVORITE PLACE TO RELAX | | |
| THE PLACE I MOST WANT TO VISIT | | |

Fill this out again, a year from when you first filled it out. How have you changed? What stayed the same?

| DATE: | YOU | ME |
|---|---|---|
| **FAVORITE VACATION** | | |
| **FAVORITE COUNTRY** | | |
| **FAVORITE PLANET** | | |
| **FAVORITE PLACE TO RELAX** | | |
| **THE PLACE I MOST WANT TO VISIT** | | |

# LET'S COOK TOGETHER!

What would you like to eat? Do you think we can make it? I do!

**Recipe name:**_____

**What do we need to make it?**

**Draw a picture or paste a photo of your finished recipe here.**

**Was it delicious? Circle YES or NO**

Every time we talk on the phone, my nephew Jack and I share how far we've gotten on various versions of Angry Birds. Every time we hang out, my niece Clara and I talk about how we're feeling kind of "goofy."

— Meg

# WHAT ARE THE TRADITIONS AND RITUALS WE SHARE?

# HERE IS A PICTURE I DREW OF YOU:

# NOW, YOU DRAW ONE OF ME:

## How do you like to spend a rainy day?

Eating a warm bowl of soup. —Michelle H.

Napping with my cats. —Matthew B.

I like to spend a rainy day playing video games—that is it! —Teddy, 7

I love curling up on the couch with a great book and a cup of tea. I'm pretty sure that's what heaven will be! —Rachel O.

Snuggled up watching *Sesame Street* with my little man. —Jaimie C.

Reading a book, cuddling my dog, sewing something cute, NOT grading papers. —Candace M.

I like to spend it inside in my pajamas and play games and take a nap. —Madelyn, 11

Building some fantastic LEGO construction with my son. Playing dolls with my daughter. Reading with one or both of them. —Aron G.

Dancing, reading, and writing. —Clara 8

Hanging out with my dog and knitting. —Meredith D.

A fantastic rainy day for me is lounging in old sweats on my couch watching a good movie. I might have a good book nearby. —Judy S.

"I know it is wet and the sun is not sunny, but we can have lots of good fun that is funny. "

**—Dr. Seuss, *The Cat in the Hat***

Plan the perfect rainy day. Will you stay inside from breakfast to dinner? Splash in puddles until you're wet from head to toe?

Start a band using instruments you find around the house (pots and pans, a harmonica, whistles, plastic bins and spoons, etc.).

**What's the name of your band?**

**What kind of music will you play?**

**What will be your best song?**

**What kind of clothes will you wear on stage?**

The library is a wonderful place to visit! Take a field trip together and explore all the amazing books and activities at your local library. But don't just stop by and pick up a couple books—have an adventure! Play with the microfilm machine, take turns looking up silly words in the dictionary, see if any authors have your name, and THEN check out a heap of fun books and movies you can enjoy together. Write all about your magical library day here.

HERE IS A PICTURE OF ME
ON MY FIRST BIRTHDAY.

ADD A PICTURE OF YOU
ON YOUR FIRST BIRTHDAY.

Go online together and search the history of your favorite things. Where are LEGOs made? Who makes the crayons you use? Who invented Matchbox cars? Write your findings down here.

Create a masterpiece together. Find a big sheet of poster board or butcher paper. Sit on opposite sides, and begin drawing, painting, pasting, and more. No need to coordinate; work at the same time, doing whatever you want. Here's the catch: Set a timer. Every ten minutes, rotate your creation by ninety degrees, and then begin work on that part. Once you've made a full rotation, see where you are…if you want to keep going, do another round. When you're finished, hang your beautiful creation where you both can see it.

If you could have any pet, what would it be? Use this page to draw your dream pets. Give them names (Rover! Felix!) and personalities (likes to watch cartoons; likes to drink cereal milk).

Fill this page with all the things that make you happy. Take turns adding one happy thing at a time (Kittens! Raisins! Hugs from Grandma!).

Visit your local art museum together. What are your favorite pieces of art?
Draw them here.

## MY FAVORITE PIECE OF ART:

YOUR FAVORITE PIECE OF ART:

# TODAY, I AM MAKING WISHES FOR YOU. I WISH....

# TODAY, YOU ARE MAKING WISHES FOR ME. WHAT DO YOU WISH?

Create an alphabet for the other person. For each letter, write a word (or more!) that describes the other person. (For example, "A" might equal agile, amazing, apple-eater).

**Here's my alphabet for you:**

Now you fill in an alphabet for me:

## What's your favorite holiday? What makes it your favorite?

Christmas! Because it is a three week celebration at my house. Lots of cookies and singing. —Angela G.

Easter because I get money and treats and rings from the Easter bunny. —Delia, 6

My birthday. Is that a holiday? —Candace M.

Halloween—I like to see everyone's creative, funny costumes. —Ruth E.

Am I allowed to say that I count the season premiere of my favorite TV show as a holiday? —Kerry S.

I love Mother's Day. A little gratitude goes a long way! We always have a fun family adventure, rain or shine! —Rachel O.

Christmas, hands down. Even though it involves a lot of stress. Watching people (kids especially) open gifts (even on FaceTime) that you chose for them and seeing that they REALLY liked them is great. —Karen K.

Pie Day. Pie is delicious, and eating pie with friends at a party makes it taste even better than usual. —Jenny C.

Um, Mickey Mouse and Donald Duck, and Christmas! I want to go to Christmas! —Zoe, 3

St. Patrick's Day because it's close to my birthday. —Jack, 6

Summer vacation. Does that count as a holiday? Nothing beats an entire summer hanging out with the kids by the pool and at Kings Island. —Tina L.

Pick out your favorite parts of every holiday (Swimming on the 4th of July! Grandpa's special apple pie for Thanksgiving!) and create a new holiday that includes the best bits. Name the holiday and all the ways you'll celebrate it here.

## ON A PERFECT SUMMER DAY,
## GO ON A PERFECT PICNIC!

Make your favorite sandwiches ahead of time, and make sure you bring enough food so you can hang out for a while. Grab a blanket, Frisbee, books to read, and find that perfect spot of green grass. *If it's winter, just camp out on your living room floor!

Get a book on face painting from the library (or look up tutorials online). Now practice turning each other into tigers and flowers and pirates. Paste pictures of your best work here.

This chart is a choose-your-own! This time, you get to fill in the topics and the answers. Have fun!

| DATE: | YOU | ME |
|---|---|---|
| | | |
| | | |
| | | |
| | | |
| | | |

Fill this out again, a year from when you first filled it out. Use the same topics as last time. How have you changed? What stayed the same?

| DATE: | YOU | ME |
|-------|-----|-----|
|       |     |    |
|       |     |    |
|       |     |    |
|       |     |    |
|       |     |    |

# CREATE A TIME CAPSULE. INSIDE, ADD:

**1.** Today's newspaper

**2.** A recent picture of you both

**3.** A letter to yourself in one year

**4.** A list of your favorite songs

**5.** A list of your top five favorite movies

**6.** One prediction about yourself that you hope will come true in a year

Decide when you're going to open it and write the date here:

List or draw the items you'll include in your time capsule here.

## Afterword

You did it! You wrote a book together, and I just know it came out great.

Meg and I wrote this book because we needed this book. We have Little Yous who we love to pieces—but we don't get to see them all the time. My niece and nephew live in Florida, but I'm in New York! My little buddy Matthew (my favorite *Star Wars* fan) lives in Washington, DC—that's closer, but still not close enough. And even the Little Yous who live nearby are so busy! It's hard to find time to get together and have fun and be silly.

My hope is that *The Big Me, Little You Book* helped you find time—over days or weeks or months—for all those good things. I hope you asked each other interesting questions, worked on fun projects, and took surprise field trips. I hope you got messy with paint and markers, and laughed like crazy watching funny movies. I hope that you learned all sorts of neat and surprising things about each other as you made your way from page one to page 200!

If you liked the book and had fun working on it together, please don't stop! Figure out what you liked doing the most (Crafts? Surveys? Reading together?) and keep doing it! Finishing this book is only the beginning—now it's up to you to keep thinking up new projects and adventures to do together. I know you'll have heaps and heaps of fun.

—Rachel

P.S. If you had fun working on this book, please let us know! We'd love to hear which bits were your favorite and to see how your projects turned out! You can always reach us at: thehappybook@gmail.com.

# Acknowledgments

Thanks to our always classy editor Shana Drehs and the rest of the Sourcebooks team for being thoughtful and enthusiastic supporters of our work.

Thanks to our agent and friend Michael Bourret who is just darn good people.

Thanks to our friends and family for sharing their ideas in our surveys.

## About the Authors

Rachel Kempster and Meg Leder are the authors of *The Happy Book*, *The Secret Me Book*, and *The You and Me Book*. They live in New York City. For more information, see http://megandrachel.tumblr.com/

Goodbye.